My RHINO Plays the XYLOPHONE

First published 2014 by A & C Black,
an imprint of Bloomsbury Publishing Plc
50 Bedford Square
London WC1B 3DP
Bloomsbury is a registered trademark of Bloomsbury Publishing Plc

www.bloomsbury.com

ISBN 978-14729-0456-0

A CIP catalogue for this book is available from the British Library.

Printed and Bound by CPI Group (UK) Ltd, Croydon CR0 4YY

1 3 5 7 9 10 8 6 4 2

My RHINO Plays the XYLOPHONE

Graham Denton

Illustrated by
Sean Longcroft

A & C BLACK
AN IMPRINT OF BLOOMSBURY
LONDON   NEW DELHI   NEW YORK   SYDNEY

For Dianna, the first port of call
when any poem puts to sea.

Contents

My Rhino Plays The Xylophone

My rhino plays the xylophone,
my tiger plays the flute,
my lemur picks a lyre
and my llama plucks a lute,
my panda has a mandolin
it delicately strums,
my elephant's a trumpeter,
my dromedary drums.

My mole knows the viola
and my antelope sitar,
my goat's a virtuoso
on a classical guitar,
my cello-playing jellyfish
is certain to astound,
my marmoset's marimba
makes a most melodic sound.

My snake can shake a rattle
and my panther bangs a gong,
my wallaby starts singing
and my ants all chant along,
my crocodile on glockenspiel
is wonderful to hear,
my weasel when it whistles
is so easy on the ear.

My lizard is a wizard
on the tenor saxophone,
my yak can play the zither,
my macaque the slide trombone,
my walrus roars in chorus
with my mongoose, moose and mouse…
if you're a fan of music
you'd just love it at my house.

I Think I'm Allergic To Mornings

I think I'm allergic to mornings.
As soon as I crawl out of bed,
I wander around like a zombie
that's just risen up from the dead.

I'm dozy, I'm dreamy, I'm drowsy,
I'm in an unshakable daze,
I stagger about in a stupor,
and cannot break out of my haze.

I'm ever so sluggish and slothful,
I'm tired from my head to my toe,
I find that I move very slowly
and haven't much get up and go.

This allergy's most disconcerting,
though, strangely, it seems, as a rule,
it only affects me on weekdays
when I'm getting ready for school.

The Spinach Went Spinning

The spinach went spinning,
the fennel was flung,
the rocket got launched
and the broccoli slung,
the radishes reeled
as the carrots were hurled,
the watercress wheeled
while the celery whirled.

Some peppers sped past
at a very fast pace,
a cucumber whacked me
smack-bang in my face,
I ducked down to dodge
an onrushing romaine…
I don't think I'll ask for
tossed salad again.

The Mouse On My Computer

The mouse on my computer's so annoying.
It will not work the way I wish it would.
But, still, I'll keep this mouse on my computer—
the hamster wasn't nearly half as good.

I'm Thinking Of Joining A Virtual Gym

I'm thinking of joining a virtual gym.
It's virtually certain to get me in trim.
I'll learn every virtual fitness technique
for reaching my virtual physical peak.

As part of my virtual training routine,
I'll go on a virtual rowing machine,
I'll put in the miles on my virtual bike,
round virtual circuits I'll virtually hike.

My virtual workouts are sure to be fun.
I'll virtually walk and I'll virtually run.
Depending how often I virtually move,
my overall virtual strength will improve.

There isn't a virtual membership fee,
my virtual gym will be virtually free.
I access my laptop…that's virtually it—
How healthy I'll feel when I'm virtually fit.

Rabbits

What do rabbits do a lot?
End up in the stewing pot!

That, or flat against the road
(don't they know their Highway Code?);

or they're always on the run,
haring from a hunter's gun.

Lucky, then, their foremost habit's
manufacturing more rabbits!

A Grape, When Flattened

A grape, when flattened by a train,
displayed the faintest sign of pain;
it lay there on the railway line
and just let out a little whine.

I Do Not Like The Darkness

I do not like the darkness.
I hate the dead of night.
I crave illumination
and hanker after light.
I pray the stars are glowing.
I hope the moon is full.
The duskiness disturbs me.
I loathe it if it's dull.

When evening throws its shadows
I'm pitched into the murk.
At once I feel uneasy.
My worries go to work.
I'm quick to get the jitters.
I flinch at every bump.
A murmur leaves me twitchy.
A whisper makes me jump.

The instant there's a blackout
I have the urge to flee.
I sense a fog descending
through which I cannot see.
My apprehension's endless.
I'm gripped by constant fear.
I find the silence eerie.
I'm scared of all I hear.

As soon as it is sunless
I'm plunged into despair.
It's dingy as a dungeon.
There's danger in the air.
I'm certain there are creatures
of whom I'll run afoul…
I wish that it were daytime
and I were not an owl.

It's My First Day As A Wizard

It's my first day as a wizard
and it isn't going well,
I've made grave miscalculations
every time I've cast a spell.

I've turned teacups into turnips,
I've turned saucers into sand,
there's an elephant before me
where a wardrobe used to stand.

When I've whispered invocations
I've changed chair legs into cheese,
and converted father's shoes
into a swarm of buzzing bees.

What was once my mother's toothbrush
has become a bowler hat.
I have put a lasting hex
upon the next-door-neighbours' cat.

My erroneous incantations
are the source of great alarm;
with each magic word I mutter
I keep causing further harm.

Now I'm clearly sprouting antlers
a reverse spell's needed fast—
or my first day as a wizard
may turn out to be my last.

A Ghost At A Party

A ghost at a party
starts singing the blues,
it lets out a yelp
and it loudly boohoos,
it cries and it sighs
and it sobs and it squalls,
it blubbers its heart out
and bellows and bawls.

A ghost at a party
it grumbles and groans,
it chants lamentations,
it mopes and it moans,
it whoops and it weeps
and it whimpers and whines,
it frets and regrets
and it rues and repines.

A ghost at a party
it hollers and howls,
it screams and it screeches,
it yells and it yowls,
then says to its host,
'This is simply sublime—
I really am having
a *wail* of a time.'

I Think My Teacher's Wonderful

I think my teacher's wonderful,
I think my teacher's ace;
she brightens up the classroom and
she lights up every face.

Her lessons are so special,
they're a pleasure to attend;
she makes the days so memorable
I wish they'd never end.

She truly is astonishing,
a jewel that's very rare;
a unique individual
who's quite beyond compare.

Of all the teachers in the school
my teacher rates the best—
at least that's what I'll tell her
just before she grades my test.

I've Pegged A Fried Egg To The Table

I've pegged a fried egg to the table
and firmly affixed the French fries,
I've fastened the fruit and the fritters,
I've padlocked the peas and the pies.
I've jammed tight the jam tarts and jelly,
the chicken and cheesecake I've latched,
I've made sure to pin the pancetta,
the salad is safely attached.

The steak has a stake through its middle,
I've stapled the grapes and the greens,
I've made sure to skewer the strudel
and nail on the plate full of beans.
The tuna's now truly unyielding,
the cucumber can't be unscrewed…
Whenever it comes to a mealtime,
I so love to bolt down my food.

A Hummingbird's A *Humming* Bird

A hummingbird's a *humming* bird—
it never sings a song.
When feathered friends are chorusing,
it never sings along.

It doesn't ever serenade,
it doesn't ever croon,
you'll never hear one warbling
or belting out a tune.

No, hummingbirds will only hum
for, unlike other birds,
as soon as they begin to sing…
they just forget the words!

My Arithmetic's Appalling

My arithmetic's appalling,
it's astonishingly bad,
I feel baffled by subtractions,
I'm quite addled when I add.
I am thoroughly befuddled
when confronted with a sum,
totting up an easy total
I'm as clueless as they come.

With all basic calculations
I don't know where to begin,
I find algebraic equations
send my head into a spin.
Logarithms make me fractious,
long division has me vexed,
if I have to tackle fractions
I'm perpetually perplexed.

Probability's a problem
that I simply can't surmount,
and an abacus is vital
should I ever try to count.
Number theory leaves me flummoxed,
I can't get to grips with graphs…
it's really hard to figure out
why I am teaching Maths.

A Top Mountaineer

Reflected a top mountaineer:
'I've had a successful career.
Alas, as I plummet
from off this high summit,
I guess it's all downhill from here.'

My Dinosaur, Dining

My dinosaur, dining, was such a disgrace,
he loved nothing better than stuffing his face,
he'd guzzle and gobble and swiftly dispatch
as much as he could down his gigantic hatch.

My dinosaur, dining, was most impolite,
to see how he feasted was no pretty sight,
he'd polish off meals and would eat like a horse,
demolishing course after course after course.

My dinosaur, dining, was ever so rude,
his manners were awful, his etiquette crude,
he'd never eat slowly, he'd overindulge,
he'd cram and he'd jam 'til his belly would bulge.

My dinosaur's vanished—my mother got tough,
she said he was banished—enough was enough!
I dine with a brother now *much* less refined...
I really do miss how my dinosaur dined.

Said A Duck, When Buying Lipstick

Said a duck, when buying lipstick,
as she took it to the till:
'I have neither cash nor credit...
please just put it on my bill.'

O Lion, Lazy Lion

O lion, lazy lion,
you're such an idle beast,
of all the creatures on the earth
you exercise the least.
You while your precious time away
in permanent repose,
asleep for twenty hours a day
(the other four, you doze).

You're famed for your complacency,
your name is world-renowned—
the reigning king of layabouts
you've rightfully been crowned.
Existing in a blissful state
of everlasting rest,
your daily recreation is
occasional at best.

Your pace is always leisurely,
your life is one of ease,
you revel in your lethargy,
and act just as you please.
To loaf about and lounge around
is all you yearn to do—
O lion, lazy lion,
O how I envy you.

I Eat Off A Plate With Four Corners

I eat off a plate with four corners

so now, in a roundabout way,

at breakfast, at lunch and at dinner

I get a square meal every day.

Haunting Sounds

Haunting sounds which get you quaking,
ghostly screams and ghastly groans,
wraithlike sounds that set you shaking,
eerie squeals and mournful moans.
Sounds of scary night-time creatures,
howling werewolves, shrieking bats,
cackling demons' high-pitched screeches,
wailing witches, keening cats.

Panic-stricken cries of terror,
mummies rapping at your door,
rattling chains and yowls of horror,
shrill and chilling sounds galore.
Creaking floorboards, footsteps creeping,
voices from beyond the grave...
When they're having trouble sleeping
that's what infant monsters crave.

My Neighbourhood Is Strange Today

My neighbourhood is strange today,
it's really very weird,
all traces of existence have
completely disappeared.
There's no familiar faces
that I usually would meet,
you'd think I was the only person
living in this street.

I feel as though I've woken
in some mystifying place,
or must have been abducted
by a ship from outer space.
I've walked around the block eight times
but haven't passed a soul—
it's like this on the days I take
my tiger for a stroll.

A Pig Has A Habit

A pig has a habit
of letting things slip.

He finds it a struggle
to button his lip.

Your innermost secrets
he's sure to reveal—

a pig cannot help it,
a pig loves to squeal.

I'm Talented At Everything

I'm talented at everything,
there's nothing I can't do,
I can play the ukulele,
I can paddle a canoe.
I'm adept at stamp collecting,
I have mastered martial arts,
I'm an expert roller skater,
I'm a champion at darts.

If you watch me when I'm boxing
you'd be truly knocked for six,
I've a flair for baton twirling
and performing magic tricks.
I can snowboard, I can snorkel,
I can skydive, I can ski,
when it comes to fossil hunting
there are none as skilled as me.

I can learn a foreign language
and it only takes a week,
I write quite exciting novels,
and my poems are unique.
I can do a thousand sit-ups,
I can juggle, I can jog,
I can sing entire operas
while I walk the neighbour's dog.

I've a knack for ballet dancing,
I've an aptitude for chess,
should I tackle origami
it's a guaranteed success.
My ability's unlimited,
my know-how never ends—
I simply cannot fathom
why I haven't any friends.

My Brother Is Nutty

My brother is nutty,
my brother is mad,
he's really not right in the head.

My brother has given up
biting his nails…
he chews on his thumbtacks instead.

I Can Never Get Down From My Camel

I can never get down from my camel.
I keep constantly coming unstuck.
And it's clear to me I'm
merely wasting my time—
you can only get *down* from a duck!

I Took My Teddy Bear To Lunch

I took my teddy bear to lunch,
but not a morsel did he munch—
whatever he was offered, he rebuffed.

He sat there and he never ate
a scrap from off his dinner plate…
I wish my teddy wasn't always stuffed.

I Once Had A Twenty-Pound Parrot

I once had a twenty-pound parrot
that used to do nothing but chat.
I found the solution to cure it…
I now have a thirty-pound cat.

My Skunk Is Not Itself Today

My skunk is not itself today,
there must be something wrong.
It's emanating pleasant smells
and lost its pungent pong.
Its odour's so adorable
my nostrils long to sniff
and get a heady waft
of its intoxicating whiff.

It smells of melted chocolate
and the sweetest-smelling bread.
It smells of cherry blossom
and new sheets upon a bed.
It's redolent of roses
when the summer's in full bloom,
and has the rich aroma
of luxurious perfume.

My skunk now has a fragrance
that is utterly divine.
I know no other skunk with such
a fine bouquet as mine.
Though clueless to the reason
for these unforeseen events,
I love it that my skunk, for once,
is making perfect scents.

A Chicken Laid An Orange

A chicken laid an orange,
which she boastfully displayed,
then beckoned to her baby chicks:
'Hey, look what marmalade!'

I Tried It In A Pair Of Shorts

I tried it in a pair of shorts—
it clasped me on the palm.
I garbed it in some overalls—
it grasped onto an arm.
I clad it in a baseball cap—
it clung with all its might.
I robed it in an anorak—
it hung on very tight.

I decked it in a sweater
and I got a nasty nip.
I next threw on a cardigan—
it fortified its grip.
I put it in pyjamas
but it clearly wasn't pleased.
I draped it with a dressing gown—
how forcefully it squeezed!

I clothed it in an overcoat—
I felt its pincers pinch.
It donned a dinner jacket
then it gave me such a clinch.
I made it wear a tracksuit—
Boy, those claws can really grab…
I think I need some lessons
in how best to dress a crab.

My Sister Is Terribly Seasick

My sister is terribly seasick,
the symptoms are there to be seen,
her face is a curious colour,
it's turning increasingly green.
She's come over truly light-headed
and seems to be losing control,
when walking, she's very unsteady—
she looks like a newly-born foal.

It's clear from my sister's appearance
she's really not feeling too well,
she's ever so pallid and pasty
and needs to lie down for a spell.
The ocean is making her queasy,
the motion of being afloat…
I so hate to think what she'll be like
the moment she steps on the boat.

A Glow Worm's Truly Fortunate

A glow worm's truly fortunate.
She grows up in the knowledge
she doesn't have to go to school
or put herself through college.
And though she won't know how to read
or ever learn to write,
however dumb she might become
she'll still be very bright.

Misleading Reading

Miss said, 'Don't scribble on the desk,'
so I, while smiling sweetly,
replied, 'I am not scribbling, Miss—
you'll find I'm writing neatly!'

A Bulky Parcel Came Today

A bulky parcel came today...
my parents' birthday present.
And judging by the parcel's shape
I'm guessing it's a pheasant.

A pheasant's not the greatest shock—
each year upon this day,
my mum and dad are always glad
to give the game away.

Septimus Grayling

As a glassblower, Septimus Grayling
had a rather regrettable failing.
When they laid him to rest,
he'd a *pane* in his chest—
'stead of blowing, he kept on inhaling!

Fear Of...

Fear of witches,
fear of germs,
fear of thunder,
fear of worms,
fear of speaking
on the phone,
fear of being
on my own,

fear of fire,
fear of smells,
fear of falling
into wells,
fear of needles,
fear of bees,
fear of fever
and disease,

fear of dentists,
fear of cold,
fear of growing
very old,
fear of failure
or defeat,
fear of walking
down the street,

fear of darkness,
fear of heights,
fear of flashing
traffic lights,
fear of shadows,
fear of sleep,
fear of swimming
out too deep,

fear of leaving
doors ajar,
fear of riding
in a car,
fear of mirrors,
fear of birds,
fear of elon-
gated words,

fear of spiders,
fear of books,
fear of getting
funny looks…
all are fears
with which I'm stricken—
guess that's why
my nickname's 'Chicken'!

I Got A Letter In The Post

I got a letter in the post.
I think it's from a friend,
but cannot pick it up because
it says, 'Please do not bend.'

I'm The World's Greatest Liar

I'm the world's greatest liar,
the best of them all,
the tales that I tell
are the tallest of tall.
Adept at deception,
I dupe and deceive,
whatever I utter
you shouldn't believe.

I fib and I fake
and I'm famed for my lies,
there's no competition—
I'm claiming the prize!
I'm wholly dishonest,
I'm so insincere,
for pure fabrication
no other comes near.

The king of baloney,
yes, that's what I am,
a fraud and a phony,
a champion sham.
I'm the world's greatest liar,
and how do I know?
A green hippopotamus
once told me so.

A Not-So-High Spirit

Our house, it seems, is playing host
to what must be a baby ghost,
for when it's flying through the air
that spook requires a boo-ster chair!

Do Excuse Me

'Do excuse me, when I beat you,'
said the dragon to the knight,
'if I choose then not to eat you,
for I have no appetite.

I don't mean to seem ungrateful.
Please don't think I'm being rude…
I just can't face one more plateful
of such flavourless tinned food!'

I'm Waving Goodbye To My Goose And My Grouse

I'm waving goodbye to my goose and my grouse,
my lynx and my minks and my moose and my mouse.
I'm bidding adieu to my shrew and my shark,
and ridding myself of my lizard and lark.

I'm not holding onto my hamster or hog.
I'm no longer wanting my ferret or frog.
I plan to dispense with my donkey and doe.
My clam and my lamb and my ram can now go.

My auk and my hawk I don't need any more.
My hare and my mare I am showing the door.
My cow and my sow I can well live without.
My quail and my whale and my snail are all out.

My loon and raccoon I am giving away.
My elks and my whelks are not welcome to stay.
I'm having a clearout of parrots and prawns.
It's farewell to oxen and foxes and fawns.

My gnat and my cat and my rat I will banish.
My guppy and puppy I'm happy to vanish.
I'm shedding my reindeer, my rabbit, my wren,
my hedgehog, my hippo, my horse and my hen.

But badgers and beavers and bats I'll retain.
The burro, the boar and the bear can remain.
I truly would miss having creatures like these.
I've always been someone who loves keeping Bs.

I'm Trying To Draw A Dinosaur

I'm trying to draw a dinosaur,
but having no success.
You'd think I wore a blindfold
I am making such a mess.
The legs are disproportionate.
The neck is much too long.
I've given it a stumpy tail.
Its head's completely wrong.

I'm trying to draw a dinosaur.
It's proving quite a pain.
I only get so far before
I have to start again.
To draw a dinosaur you need
an awful lot of skill,
but what is more important is…
your dinosaur keeps still!

Said The Mummy

Said the Mummy, 'I'm starting to find
that this job is a bit of a bind.
Though I'm white as a sheet
and quite dead on my feet,
I just don't get the chance to unwind!'

My Neighbours Are Ever So Noisy

My neighbours are ever so noisy,
they're constantly at it all day,
they whistle, they warble, they whinny,
they cackle and chatter away.
The moment I open my window,
I'm greeted with grunting and growls,
my ears are assaulted by bellows,
I meet all their hoots and their howls.

The racket they make is relentless,
I haven't been sleeping a wink,
when faced with a salvo of screeching,
I hardly can hear myself think.
They chirp and they chirrup and chortle,
they crow and they croak and they creak,
I cannot ignore all their squawking,
I catch it whenever they squeak.

They're endlessly rowdy and raucous,
they yowl and they yelp and they yap,
much more of their whooping and wailing
I think I am liable to snap.
I have such cacophonous neighbours,
yet what am I going to do?
There isn't much sense in complaining—
I'm living next door to the zoo.

A Banana By The Ocean

A banana by the ocean
lay upon the golden sand,
where it bathed with great devotion
'til its skin completely tanned.

That banana by the ocean
should have kept itself concealed—
it forgot the suntan lotion
so the poor banana peeled.

Welcome To My Haunted Chamber

Welcome to my haunted chamber…
all who enter here, *beware!*
You will be in mortal danger—
cross the threshold, if you dare.
You'll encounter gruesome creatures
who intend to do you harm,
grisly fiends with ghoulish features
guaranteed to cause alarm.

You will witness ghostly visions,
sights to scare you half to death,
nasty, ghastly apparitions
that'll take away your breath.
There are deadly beasts residing,
presences that lie in wait,
spectres who'll come out of hiding,
ready to decide your fate.

Weird and eerie beings will greet you,
it won't be a lot of fun,
lest you wish them all to eat you,
I would recommend you run.
Should you fail to heed this warning,
it is sure to mean your doom—
that's what I tell Mum each morning
when she wants to clean my room.

A Rat Whose Teeth

A rat whose teeth once caused it pain
now has no reason to complain—
the dentist that he went to see
was practiced in rodentistry.

I'm Dining Out On Brussels Sprouts

I'm dining out on Brussels sprouts,
on broccoli and bran,
I'm eating all the sauerkraut
and sausages I can.

I binged upon baked beans last night,
plus prunes in syrup (tinned)—
today I'd like to fly my kite…
I thought I'd need the wind.

Pupil Troubles

There once was a teacher, Miss Wright,
whose lessons affected her sight.
Through all of her classes
she sported dark glasses—
her students were simply too bright!

I Ate A Clove Of Garlic

I ate a clove of garlic,
then I gobbled down one more,
I gorged upon a third, before
I guzzled number four.
A fifth and sixth were followed
by cloves seven, eight and nine,
but when a tenth I'd swallowed,
well, I had to draw the line.

My stomach's feeling dreadful,
and my breath is quite the worst,
I have an awful headache,
I just cannot quench my thirst.
I ate ten cloves of garlic
but at least I've now no fear—
of Grandma's goodnight kisses
or of vampires coming near.

When Porcupines Play Volleyball

When porcupines play volleyball,
the games are always short.
It's safe to say it doesn't make
a great spectator sport.

No sooner has a shot been made
the action has to stop—
the moment that the ball is played
it goes off with a POP!

And when they try a second time
it ends just like the first—
it only takes one shot before
the volleyball is burst.

For though it is a game that they
unquestionably like…
when porcupines play volleyball
they only ever *spike*.

My Brother's Incredibly Ugly

My brother's incredibly ugly,
you won't see a scarier sight,
he looks like a heavyweight bruiser
who's come off much worse in a fight.
His phizog is no pretty picture,
I recommend turning away,
one glimpse of his hideous visage
is certain to ruin your day.

Whenever I glance at my brother,
I instantly let out a yelp,
it's truly a nightmarish vision,
I have to go running for help.
I cannot believe we're related,
it's hard to admit we are kin—
but mostly I feel so unlucky
that he's my identical twin.

Will Someone Fetch The Garden Shears

Will someone fetch the garden shears—
there's roses growing from my ears!
Of all the luck, of all the ills...
I thought I'd planted daffodils!

My Dog Keeps Chewing Up The Couch

My dog keeps chewing up the couch,
I don't know what to do,
he never chews on anything
a dog's supposed to chew.

I give my dog a rubber ball,
I give my dog a bone,
I give my dog my slippers—
he just leaves them well alone.

I give my dog a plastic toy,
it doesn't do the trick.
A pair of shoes my dog eschews,
he never chews a stick.

I teach my dog obedience
yet nothing seems to work…
my doggie sees the sofa and
my doggie goes berserk.

He'll grip it and he'll rip it
and he'll nibble and he'll gnaw—
there's stuffing strewn all over
and there's fluff upon the floor.

It's obvious this couch is all
my doggie wants to eat—
I guess I'm best accepting it…
his tooth is very suite.

I Think I've Invented A Colour

I think I've invented a colour,
a colour that's never been seen,
it isn't a red or an orange,
it isn't a yellow or green.
It's neither a lime nor a lemon,
nor is it a purple or blue,
this colour is totally novel,
this colour is perfectly new.

I think I've invented a colour,
that's almost too hard to define,
there's no other colour I know of
that looks like this colour of mine.
This colour is certainly special,
a one-of-a-kind and, what's more,
it's unlike the hundreds of colours
I think I've invented before.

An Ant Upon A Jam Jar

An ant, upon a jam jar,
began to throw a strop.
He ranted, 'I'm so angry,
I'm going to blow my top!
This lid says, *Twist to open,*
it simply can't be right—
I've danced and danced and danced but still
the lid is fastened tight!'

Bread And Butter, How I Love You

Bread and butter, how I love you,
bread and butter, you're the best,
for you please me like no other,
you're so easy to digest.
You're impossible to better,
there is nothing I love more—
bread and butter, bread and butter,
you're the meal that I adore.

Bread and butter, you're delicious
you are quite beyond compare,
you're the simplest of dishes,
yet the most nutritious fare.
I could eat a zillion slices,
I could live on little but,
I am bats for bread and butter,
I'm a bread and butter nut.

Bread and butter, I'm besotted,
I have got you on my brain,
it's a phrase I always utter
and my favourite refrain.
I am positively potty,
I am utterly obsessed…
bread and butter, how I love you,
bread and butter, you're the best.

Every Time I Phone The Zoo

Every time I phone the zoo
it has me in a tizzy,
it's such a struggle getting through—
the lion's always busy.

I Am Sweating! I Am Sweating!

I am sweating! I am sweating!
like I've never done before,
it is positively pouring
out of every single pore.
There's a torrent from my forehead,
sweat is streaming down my arms,
gleaming beads of perspiration
keep appearing on my palms.

I am sweating! I am sweating!
I just cannot stem the flow,
should you fail to keep your distance
you'll be drenched from head to toe.
I am spouting like a fountain,
I am spurting like a jet,
all my clothes are clinging to me
and my skin is wringing wet.

I am sweating! I am sweating!
there are puddles at my feet,
if I carry on much longer
I'll be flooding out the street.
Oh, I'm gushing like a geyser,
I am oozing everywhere,
for I'm sweating as I'm getting
ready for the dentist's chair!

My T. Rex Is Poorly

My T. rex is poorly,
my T. rex is ill,
he's really not feeling too great.

He's under the weather
and doesn't look clever—
it must be somebody he ate!

Bear Essentials

You want to know what pet to keep?
Well, let me offer advice...
a polar bear is very cheap—
it lives on nothing but ice!

I'm A Very Snappy Dragon

I'm a very snappy dragon
and I'm in a mood today,
so be wary when you're near me
and be careful what you say.
I'm irascible by nature,
I am prickly through and through,
I'll display my indignation
at whatever you might do.

I'm notoriously grumpy,
I'm particularly gruff,
I am permanently sulky,
I am always in a huff.
You'd be wise to pacify me,
I'm ferocious when annoyed,
I can morph into a monster
I'd advise you to avoid.

I am touchy, I am tetchy,
I am quick to throw a strop,
I possess a wicked temper,
I completely blow my top.
I lack any sense of humour,
you won't ever see me smile,
I'm a picture of resentment,
with a belly full of bile.

I'm malicious and I'm vicious,
and my disposition's fierce,
I've a tongue of dripping venom,
I have talons that'll pierce.
So ignore this at your peril
for I guarantee you'll pay—
I'm a very snappy dragon
and I'm in a mood today.

Double Trouble

The Cyclops said,
'I think I must
have bumped my head
and been concussed.
I need to see
a Cycloptician—
I've now got twenty-
twenty vision!'

First Service

Here's a fact you might not know—
tennis is the oldest sport.
How exactly is that so?
Moses served in Pharaoh's court!

My Goldfish

To satisfy his dying wish
to emulate a flying fish,
I took my goldfish on a plane…
then flushed him somewhere over Spain.

Mynah Problems

The Mynah bird
has quite a gimmick—
you'll find that there's
no finer mimic.

I've heard, if taught,
one of these birds
can learn up to
a hundred words.

But, as it mocks
the things it hears,
be careful what
goes in its ears;

a Mynah's quick
to pick up speech
you likely didn't
mean to teach,

which they then go
about repeating…
and make you wish they'd
stick to tweeting.

My Cat Is In Love With The Goldfish

My cat is in love with the goldfish.
He's practically head over heels.
He cannot hold back his emotions
or mask the affection he feels.

He'll bring her big bundles of roses.
He'll give her these syrupy notes
declaring undying devotion,
embellished with cute little quotes.

He'll pen the most passionate poems
a pussy could possibly write,
then sit by her bowl in the evening
and promptly proceed to recite.

He'll whisper such sickly sweet nothings
whilst barely averting his gaze.
He'll sing serenades in her honour
whose verses are bursting with praise.

Yes, my cat's so in love with the goldfish,
yet the chances of romance are poor,
for, alas, the attraction's one-sided...
the fish loves the tabby next door.

I Took My Dog To See A Film

I took my dog to see a film—
my dog was gripped throughout;
she didn't shuffle in her seat,
she didn't kick about.

She fixed upon that picture
and she followed every scene—
not once was she distracted
from the action on the screen.

She sat there captivated
as she watched the plot unfold,
from the moment that it opened
'til the closing credits rolled.

She came out of the cinema
with such a happy look.
It's odd my dog should love that film—
she didn't like the book.

On The Very First Valentine's Day...

What the caveman gave his missus—
lots and lots of *ughs* and kisses.

I Am Huffing, I Am Puffing

I am huffing, I am puffing,
I can barely catch my breath,
I feel perilously perched upon
the verge of certain death.
I am absolutely shattered,
I am positively bushed,
I have pushed myself much further
than a human should be pushed.

I feel fit for next to nothing,
I am almost on the deck,
I'm devoid of any vigour,
I am virtually a wreck.
All my muscles are complaining,
and my legs are lumps of lead,
there's a knot inside my stomach,
I've an aching in my head.

I can hardly move an eyelid,
I've got zero left to give,
I have reached the utter limits,
I have lost my will to live.
This is when the coach announces
as he primes his starting gun,
'Right, you lot, the warm-up's over…
now it's time to start your run.'

A Bee With A Bee In Its Bonnet

There's a bee with a bee in its bonnet
that is heading incredibly near,
and I feel, to be perfectly honest,
it is better if I disappear,
for that bee with a bee in its bonnet
is quite clearly a resolute bee—
I fear that whatever his point is
he's determined to share it with me.

Mum's Umbrage

The teacher called my mother
on my first day back at school,
he claimed that I'd been wayward
and behaving like a fool.

'Now just you wait a moment,'
came my mother's quick response,
'he misbehaved all summer
and I never called *you* once!'

Persevering Percival

I am Persevering Percival,
relentless in my quest,
my thirst is quite unquenchable,
I never let things rest.
I'm gritty and I'm merciless,
I'm firm and resolute,
I persist when others weaken,
and stay fixed in my pursuit.

I'm a dogged individual,
I do what I intend.
I'm unshakeable, unbreakable,
you cannot make me bend.
I am stubborn, staunch and steadfast,
for I have a one-track mind,
and to what does not concern me
I am absolutely blind.

I am totally unyielding,
as tenacious as can be,
there is no one so decisive
and unwavering as me.
Yes, I'm Persevering Percival,
resolved to see things through...
if I only could determine
what it is I'm going to do.

My Teacher Grew Quite Furious

My teacher grew quite furious,
he flew into a rage,
when the homework that I passed him
had no words upon the page.

'*If I owned a million dollars...*'
is what Teacher had us write,
which is why I handed over
just the blankest sheet of white.

'You've done *nothing!*' Teacher hollered.
'Yes,' I told him, 'that is true—
if I owned a million dollars,
that's *exactly* what I'd do!'

I Wonder

I wonder
if under
a witch's

h____   ____t

her head is really shaped like that?

Silk Tie

Two silk worms had a race.
But neither won the chase.
And here's the reason why:
they ended in a tie.

Index of First Lines

Acknowledgements

'A Top Mountaineer' first appeared as 'A Bit Of A Low Point' in *Read Me And Laugh*, chosen by Gaby Morgan, Macmillan 2005.

'Do Excuse Me' first appeared in *GRRR!*, James Carter and Graham Denton, Macmillan 2013.

'First Service' first appeared in *When Granny Won Olympic Gold: And Other Medal-Winning Poems*, chosen by Graham Denton, A&C Black 2012.

'I Am Huffing, I Am Puffing' first appeared in *When Granny Won Olympic Gold: And Other Medal-Winning Poems*, chosen by Graham Denton, A&C Black 2012.

'I Took My Dog To See A Film' first appeared as 'I Took My Dog To A Movie' in *Laugh Out Loud!* Funny Poems chosen by Fiona Waters, Macmillan 2008.

'I Wonder' first appeared as 'A Point Worth Raising' in *Wizard Poems*, chosen by Fiona Waters, Macmillan 2004.

'I'm A Very Snappy Dragon' first appeared in *GRRR!*, James Carter and Graham Denton, Macmillan 2013.

'Misleading Reading' first appeared in *The Dog Ate My Buspass*: Poems Chosen by Nick Toczek and Andrew Fusek Peters, Macmillan 2004.

'Mum's Umbrage' first appeared in *The Jumble Book*: Poems Chosen by Roger Stevens, Macmillan 2009.

'My Cat Is In Love With The Goldfish' first appeared in *My Cat Is In Love With The Goldfish*, chosen by Graham Denton, A&C Black 2010.

'My Dinosaur, Dining' first appeared in *GRRR!*, James Carter and Graham Denton, Macmillan 2013.

'My T. Rex Is Poorly' first appeared in *GRRR!*, James Carter and Graham Denton, Macmillan 2013.

'My Teacher Grew Quite Furious' first appeared as 'Nothing Doing' in *Laugh Out Loud!* Funny Poems chosen by Fiona Waters, Macmillan 2008.

'Mynah Problems' first appeared in *Wild!: Rhymes that Roar*, chosen by James Carter and Graham Denton, Macmillan 2009.

'On The Very First Valentine's Day…' first appeared in *My Cat Is In Love With The Goldfish*, chosen by Graham Denton, A&C Black 2010.

'Persevering Percival' first appeared in *Laugh Out Loud!* Funny Poems chosen by Fiona Waters, Macmillan 2008.

'Pupil Troubles' first appeared in *Read Me At School*, chosen by Gaby Morgan, Macmillan 2009.

'Rabbits' first appeared in *The RSPB Anthology Of Wildlife Poetry*, selected by Celia Warren, A&C Black 2011.

'Said The Mummy' first appeared as 'All The Trappings' in *Monster Poems*, chosen by Brian Moses, Macmillan 2005.

'Septimus Grayling' first appeared as 'What A Sucker!' in *Shouting At The Ocean: Poems Chosen by Graham Denton, Andrea Shavick and Roger Stevens*, Hands Up Books 2009.

'Silk Tie' first appeared in *When Granny Won Olympic Gold: And Other Medal-Winning Poems,* chosen by Graham Denton, A&C Black 2012.